My Kurdish Community

Kate Taylor and Dlawa Sarbest

Photography by Chris Fairclough

FRANKLIN WATTS
LONDON•SYDNEY

First published in 2005 by
Franklin Watts
96 Leonard Street
London
EC2A 4XD

Franklin Watts Australia
45-51 Huntley Street
Alexandria
NSW 2015

ISBN: 0 7496 5878 9

A CIP catalogue record for this book
is available from the British Library

Printed in Malaysia
Planning and production by Discovery Books Limited
Editor: Laura Durman
Designer: Ian Winton

The author, packager and publisher would like to thank the following people
for their participation in this book:
    Dlawa's family, with special thanks to Sarbest
    Dlawa's friends, Candice, Basit and Amy
    The KCC
    Broadwater Primary School
    Head Teacher Mr Shepheard
    Al-Muntada newspaper
    Oli Centre
    Fresh Food City

Photo acknowledgements: Art Directors / Ask Images, page 11

Contents

All About Me

My name is Dlawa Sarbest and I'm nine years old. I am *Kurdish*.

I live in London, in a area called Tooting. Quite a lot of Kurds live in London.

I am a *Muslim*, but I don't go to a *mosque* to pray like lots of other Muslims do.

I live in a house with my 5-year-old sister, Deanna, and my mum and dad.

▶ **My family outside our house.**

I have my own room and my sister shares a room with my parents.

◀ **This is my bedroom.**

My Family

I have relatives in many countries, but some of my family live in London too.

My mum is called Dlikosh, and my dad is called Sarbest. They are both from *Kurdistan*.

▲ **Me with my parents and sister.**

My mum moved to London twenty years ago. She's a professional singer and sells her CDs all over the world. My dad has lived here for 15 years. He writes poetry in his spare time, and used to play football professionally in Iraq.

My Aunt Pary and Uncle Kadir live nearby with my cousin Laveen. She's only 1 year old. We see her a lot, and she's really sweet.

▲ My aunt, uncle and cousin.

◀ Me with Laveen.

7

Where I Live

I like Tooting. I've lived here all my life.

▶ **I live in this road.**

I can play out in our road with my friends because it's really quiet.

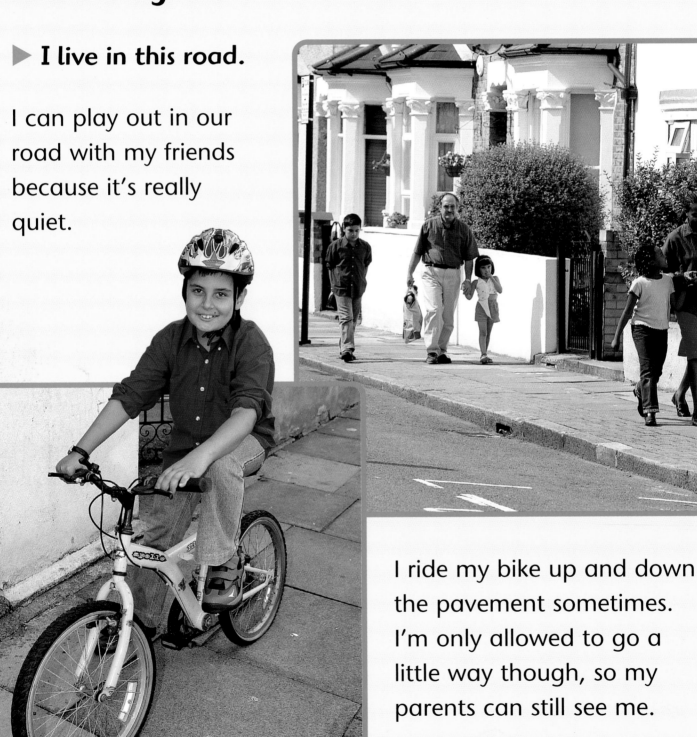

I ride my bike up and down the pavement sometimes. I'm only allowed to go a little way though, so my parents can still see me.

My favourite park is called Tooting Common Park. It's good because you can play in the playground and watch people playing tennis at the same time. I love tennis.

▲ **Me with Deanna at the park.**

My Homeland

Kurdistan is my homeland. It's not a state; it's split between the countries called Iraq, Turkey, Syria and Iran.

My mum and dad talk to me about Kurdistan quite a lot. I have been there on holiday twice: once when I was 3 years old, and again when I was 7.

▲ The Kurdish flag.

▶▼ These maps show where Kurdistan is.

EUROPE

ASIA

Kurdistan

AFRICA

ARMENIA

AZERBAIJAN

TURKEY

Bingol • • Mus

Bitlis • • Van

Diyarbakir • Siirt • • Sirnak

Al-Qamishli •

Al-Hasakah • Al Mawsil • • Mahabad

• Arbil

Kirkuk • • As Sulaymaniyah

SYRIA

IRAN

Kermanshah •

IRAQ

200 miles

200 km

I have lots of relatives who still live in Kurdistan. My grandmother lives in Kirkuk. Most of my family lives in As Sulaymaniyah though, like my dad's brother Omar.

When I was on holiday in Kurdistan, we went for lots of picnics with our family. There are mountains and rivers that are really nice to sit by. We ate things like lamb kebabs and bread.

All Kurdish people wish that Kurdistan could become a separate country.

▲ **This picture shows the lovely mountains and rivers in my homeland.**

The KCC

My dad works at a place called the Kurdish Cultural Centre, or KCC.

I go there every Saturday with lots of other Kurdish children. We learn the Kurdish language, play games, sing and have fun.

▶ My dad's office.

◀▼ We get a certificate that says how good our Kurdish is.

Every Friday lots of older people come to the centre to play games, to chat and to have lunch.

▶ **This lady is giving a talk about traditional Kurdish cooking.**

The centre also helps Kurdish people who move to England. People like my dad give them advice and support. Some of them don't speak any English so they need our help.

◀ **My dad helping someone at the KCC.**

Shops

I like going shopping with my mum, especially to Kurdish shops.

The shops closest to us are on a street called Tooting Broadway. It's huge and you can buy anything you want.

▲ **Tooting Broadway.**

There's a big supermarket where we do a lot of our food shopping, but there are some Pakistani shops where we buy food as well.

▶ **Me buying vegetables with my parents.**

▼ **I love buying freshly baked bread.**

Sometimes we travel a little further to food shops run by Kurdish people. They speak to me in Kurdish, which is nice.

My School

I go to a school called Broadwater Primary School. I really like it!

Deanna is in the reception class at my school. There aren't many other Kurdish children there though.

My favourite subject is history. I'm really interested in finding out about what happened a long time ago and learning about events all around the world.

◀ These children are in my class.

At break time we go out and play in the playground. It's nice if it's hot outside, but sometimes in the winter it's freezing.

▶ **Me playing catch in the playground.**

My mum makes me a packed lunch every day. I usually have a cheese and jam sandwich, a packet of crisps and some fruit.

▼ **Me eating lunch with my friends.**

My Friends

I have lots of friends, but my best friends are Basit, Candice and Amy.

Basit and Candice go to my school. We usually play together at break times. I've known them for about 5 years, since we started school!

▼ **Me with Basit and Candice.**

Amy lives near me, and we play together after school and at the weekends. We play lots of games. My favourite is a Kurdish game a bit like Bey Blades.

You wrap a piece of string around a wooden top and try to keep it spinning for longer than anybody else. I play with Bey Blades, too.

◀ Me playing with Amy and Deanna.

Food

My family eats Kurdish food. My favourites are lamb kebabs and *yaprak*.

For breakfast I like yogurt, *chickpeas* and walnuts. My mum heats the chickpeas up and they're delicious.

▼ **Me and Deanna having breakfast.**

My family drink a lot of tea. I have it with milk and sugar. We mix different types of tea leaves together and add *cardamom pods*.

▼ **Me picking vine leaves in the garden.**

There's a grape vine in our back garden, and at the weekends my mum sometimes makes a nice dish called yaprak. She mixes minced meat and rice with spring onions, *dill* and yogurt, and wraps it in the vine leaves.

◄ **Yaprak.**

21

My Hobbies

I have lots of different hobbies, like drawing, playing music and football.

I love riding my bike. Sometimes dad puts our bikes in the car and we go places where you can cycle for miles.

I play football with my dad too. He's really good!

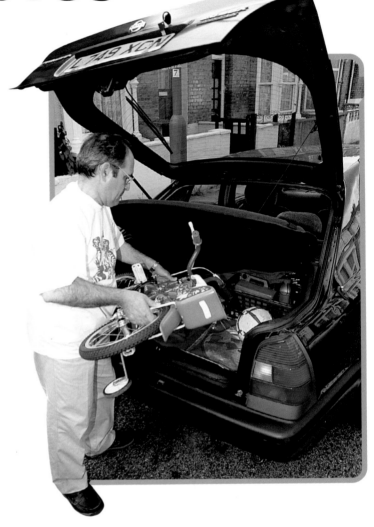

◀ Me and my dad playing football in the park.

I'm a pretty good artist. I have done hundreds of drawings and paintings, and even designed two covers for poetry books my dad has written. This is a drawing of Spiderman I did the other day. Spiderman is my favourite film. I've seen it over a hundred times!

◀ Sometimes I go rollerblading in the park. It's fun!

Languages

I speak two languages: Kurdish at home and English at school.

My parents think it's important for Deanna and me to speak Kurdish at home. They want us to remember our language from Kurdistan. I speak English at school though, because there aren't many other Kurdish children there.

▲ **My dad talking to me in Kurdish.**

My dad can speak six different languages, including Kurdish, Arabic, Turkish and English. I want to speak lots of languages when I'm older. Soon I'll be learning French at school.

► **This is our local, Kurdish newspaper.**

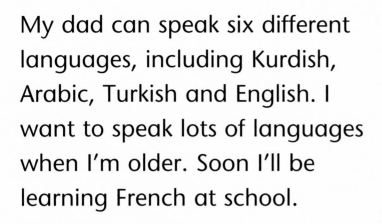

My dad wrote this poem in Kurdish. A friend of ours made it into a piece of art.

Clothes

I usually wear jeans and t-shirts at home, but I sometimes wear a *shalwar*.

A shalwar is a pair of trousers with a tunic top. If I lived in Kurdistan, I would wear this all the time but because we live in England I wear the same clothes as other English children. I usually wear a shalwar on special occasions though.

► Me with my family in our traditional Kurdish clothing.

Deanna has lots of different outfits called *krasi kurdi*. Her favourite one is orange. She loves wearing bracelets too.

▶ **Deanna choosing which bracelet to wear.**

My parents only wear Kurdish clothes on special occasions. My dad always wears a suit to work.

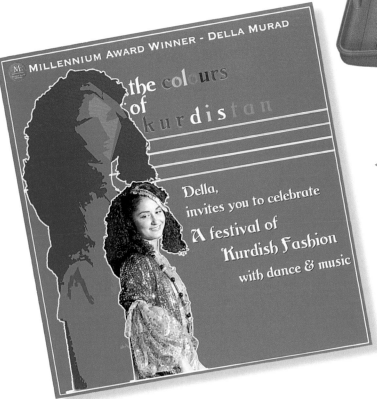

MILLENNIUM AWARD WINNER - DELLA MURAD

the colours of kurdistan

Della, invites you to celebrate
A festival of Kurdish Fashion
with dance & music

◀ **Sometimes there are Kurdish fashion shows in London. We like to go and watch. They often have Kurdish music and dancing too.**

Festivals and Music

I love music, especially singing. When we celebrate the Kurdish festival called Nowroz, there's lots of music and dancing.

◀ Children singing a special Nowroz song in the KCC.

Nowroz means Kurdish New Year. We often celebrate at the KCC with our friends. We sing special songs and wear traditional Kurdish clothing. Sometimes I get a new outfit to wear!

▶ I love singing Kurdish songs with my mum. This is one of the CDs that she's made.

1. HÎWAY JÎYAN
2. PEŞÎMANÎ
3. WERE DÊRE
4. VEGERE YAR
5. CUDAYÎ
6. KOÇ
7.
8. CEM MEHELÊ

DILXOŞ

28

I've taught myself to play the keyboard, and I'd like to learn to play a Saz as well. This is a Kurdish instrument like a guitar. People play it in folk music, and in some of my mum's songs.

Sometimes Kurdish musicians come over to London to give concerts of traditional Kurdish music. We always try to go and see them.

▶ **This is an advert for a concert I went to.**

An Evening of Kurdish Music

with
The Living Fire Ensemble

Friday 7 May
7.45pm
Queen Elizabeth Hall
Tickets - £20, £17.50
Presented by MultiCulti

Shahin Talabani   Adnan Karim

I like Tooting

I have lived in London all of my life. Although I enjoyed it when I went to Kurdistan on holiday, I think I will live here when I'm older.

Glossary

Cardamom pod Cardamom is a spice used to flavour food or drink. Each pod contains several cardamom seeds.

Chickpea A round, yellow seed from the chickpea plant.

Dill A herb used to flavour food.

Krasi kurdi The traditional costume for Kurdish women and girls. It consists of a dress, a waistcoat and a belt.

Kurdish Kurdish people come from the region called Kurdistan in Asia. Their language is also called Kurdish, and is spoken by over 30 million people around the world.

Kurdistan This is the homeland of the Kurdish people. It is a region split between the countries called Iraq, Turkey, Syria and Iran.

Mosque The building in which Muslims worship.

Muslim A person who follows the religion called Islam.

Shalwar The traditional costume for Kurdish men and boys. It consists of a pair of trousers with a tunic top.

Yaprak A traditional Kurdish dish. Minced meat, rice, spring onions, dill and yogurt are wrapped in vine leaves and cooked.

Index